Alternative Energy

Water Power

Energy from Rivers, Waves, and Tides

LAURIE BREARLEY

Children's Press®
An Imprint of Scholastic Inc.

Content Consultant
Kevin Doran, J.D., Institute Fellow and Research Professor,
Renewable and Sustainable Energy Institute,
University of Colorado at Boulder

Library of Congress Cataloging-in-Publication Data

Names: Brearley, Laurie, 1953- author.
Title: Water power : energy from rivers, waves, and tides / by Laurie Brearley.
Other titles: True book.
Description: New York, NY : Children's Press, [2018] | Series: A true book |
   Includes bibliographical references and index.
Identifiers: LCCN 2018009075| ISBN 9780531236871 (library binding) | ISBN
   9780531239445 (pbk.)
Subjects: LCSH: Water-power--Juvenile literature. | Tidal power--Juvenile
   literature. | Hydroelectric power plants--Juvenile literature. | Renewable
   energy sources--Juvenile literature.
Classification: LCC TC146 .B74 2018 | DDC 333.91/4--dc23 LC record available at
https://lccn.loc.gov/2018009075

All rights reserved. Published in 2019 by Children's Press, an imprint of Scholastic Inc.
Printed in Heshan, China 62

SCHOLASTIC, CHILDREN'S PRESS, A TRUE BOOK™, and associated logos are trademarks and/or
registered trademarks of Scholastic Inc.

Scholastic Inc., 557 Broadway, New York, NY 10012

1 2 3 4 5 6 7 8 9 10 R 28 27 26 25 24 23 22 21 20 19

Front cover: Karakaya Dam in Turkey
Back cover: Surfer

Find the Truth!

Everything you are about to read is true *except* for one of the sentences on this page.

Which one is **TRUE**?

T or F People first started using water power in the 1800s.

T or F Ocean waves are affected by the moon.

Find the answers in this book.

Contents

THE BIG TRUTH!

Affecting the Environment

Earth

Ocean wave

Ancient water clock

A Need for Alternative Energy

We use energy every day. It fuels cars and powers cell phones. It cools homes when it's hot outside and warms them when the weather turns cold. It provides light through the night while the sun shines on the other half of the world.

All this energy must come from somewhere. Since the 1700s, people have relied mostly on fossil fuels such as coal, oil, and natural gas. These materials burn easily to create heat and can be turned into electricity. But they are far from perfect.

Our supply of fossil fuels is limited. Experts predict that **fossil fuels will dwindle and their cost will rise**. In addition, **burning these fuels releases harmful substances**.

Some substances trap heat within the atmosphere, leading to **climate change**. Others cause health problems, including heart and lung diseases.

What Can We Do?

Renewable energy sources, such as solar, wind, water, and geothermal, are healthier sources than fossil fuels. They can serve our electricity needs while reducing the damage done to the planet and us.

Turn the page and learn the secrets of one of these alternative energies: water power.

The Grand Canyon is more than 1 mile (1.6 kilometers) deep at its deepest point.

CHAPTER 1

Water in Motion

The Grand Canyon in northern Arizona is one of the scenic wonders of the world. Millions of tourists come every year to see this breathtaking natural formation. But there would be nothing to see if not for water power. The Grand Canyon was carved by the rushing waters of the Colorado River. Over millions of years, the rapidly flowing water chiseled into the earth and deepened the channel into the famous steep-walled gorge of today.

Ocean shorelines often feature dramatic rock formations that have been shaped by ocean waves slamming against them.

What Makes Water Move?

From rushing streams to rolling ocean waves, many bodies of water are almost constantly in motion. This motion shapes Earth's surface. Water carries soil downhill, cutting valleys. It batters shorelines, grinding stones into sand. It seeps into rock and freezes, shattering mountains. The movement of water is powerful because it has kinetic energy. This is active, moving energy. When moving water pushes against other objects, its kinetic energy is transferred to them.

So what makes water move? Two major causes are the force of gravity and precipitation. Streams and rivers flow as water moves downhill across the land. The moving waters eventually drain into oceans, lakes, or even other rivers. The rivers and streams are replenished as rain or other precipitation falls from the sky. Gravity from the moon affects water, too. It pulls on Earth's water and creates the ocean's tides. People can capture the energy of this movement and use it for a variety of purposes.

Streams and rivers flow as gravity pulls water downward along sloping surfaces.

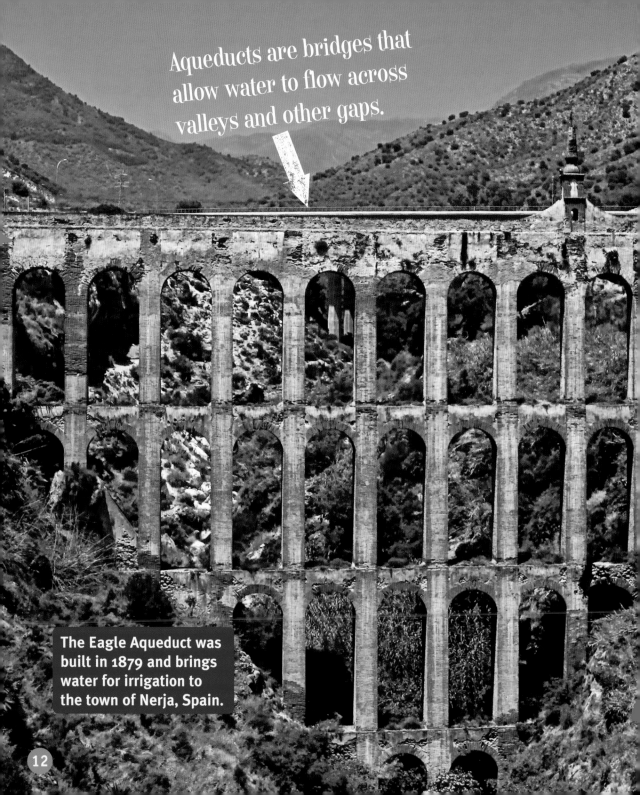

Aqueducts are bridges that allow water to flow across valleys and other gaps.

The Eagle Aqueduct was built in 1879 and brings water for irrigation to the town of Nerja, Spain.

CHAPTER 2

A Powerful History

Water has been an essential power source for thousands of years. It is used for transportation, to operate machines, and to keep our homes free of waste. Power from water is called hydropower. *Hydro* is a Greek word meaning "water." Hydropower has a lot of advantages over other power sources. It does not release harmful chemicals into the water or air. There is no pollution. And hydropower's main fuel—water—is not used up. This means it is a **renewable** energy source.

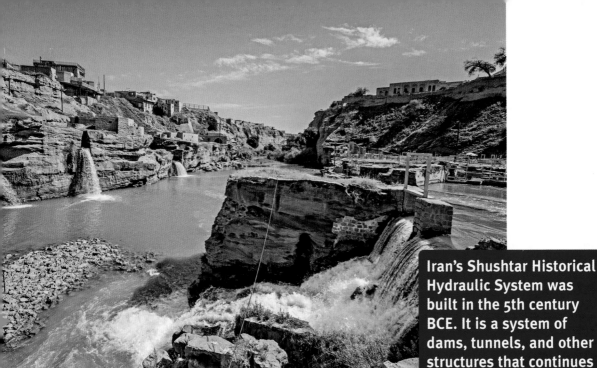

Iran's Shushtar Historical Hydraulic System was built in the 5th century BCE. It is a system of dams, tunnels, and other structures that continues to provide water to the city of Shushtar today.

Discovering Water Power

The first use humans found for water power was transportation. Ancient peoples used canoes to travel along streams and rivers. They also loaded heavy objects onto rafts and floated them downstream.

Ancient farmers relied on water power for **irrigation**. They built **canals** leading from rivers to their fields. The water flowed down the canals to the farmers' crops.

A Practical Power Source

Water power has also been used for other practical tasks. The water clock was an early timekeeping device that was invented thousands of years ago. It was shaped like a bowl, and water flowed into or out of it at a steady rate. By looking at how full the bowl was, people could determine how much time had passed since the water had started flowing.

This ancient Egyptian water clock dates back to the 14th century BCE.

Waterwheels and Water Mills

A waterwheel uses water power to do mechanical work such as grinding grain. It is a large wheel with wide paddles. As flowing water passes over the paddles, the wheel turns on an **axle**. The movement of the axle can then power a variety of machines. The Greeks and other cultures used waterwheels by at least the 1st century BCE. By the 6th century CE, water mills were common throughout Europe.

Timeline of Water Power

100 BCE
Ancient Greeks and other cultures used waterwheels for irrigation, grinding grain, and other purposes.

1882
The world's first hydroelectric power plant is built to power a paper mill in Appleton, Wisconsin.

| 100 BCE | 1700s CE | 1882 | 1894 |

1700s CE
French engineer Bernard Forest de Belidor writes *Architecture hydraulique*, a landmark work about the construction of waterwheels, pumps, and other water-powered devices.

1894
Nikola Tesla's hydroelectric station at Niagara Falls provides electricity to Buffalo, New York.

It's Electric!

Late in the 1800s, people found another use for water power: generating electricity. In 1882, the world's first hydroelectric plant began operating on Wisconsin's Fox River. It used the natural movement of the river to generate enough electricity to light up the power plant itself and two nearby buildings. Since then, the technology behind hydroelectric power plants has been greatly improved.

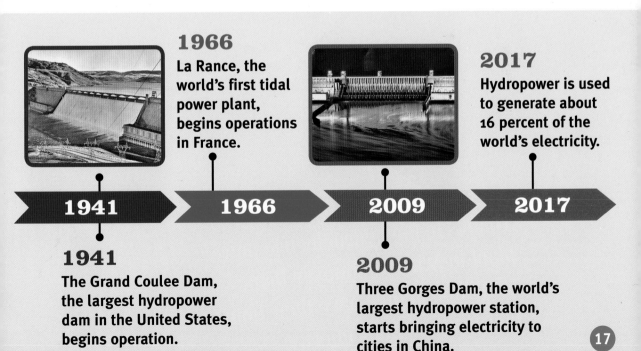

1966
La Rance, the world's first tidal power plant, begins operations in France.

2017
Hydropower is used to generate about 16 percent of the world's electricity.

1941 **1966** **2009** **2017**

1941
The Grand Coulee Dam, the largest hydropower dam in the United States, begins operation.

2009
Three Gorges Dam, the world's largest hydropower station, starts bringing electricity to cities in China.

Thanks to the hydroelectric power plant in Arizona's Hoover Dam, 1.3 million people have their homes powered by water energy.

CHAPTER **3**

From Water to Electricity

Today, there are hydroelectric power plants all around the world, making water the most widely used renewable energy source. Almost all of these plants are built into dams. A dam is a structure built across a body of running water such as a river or stream. Dams are often built to help control flooding or increase the depth of river water for navigation or recreational use. But they are also used to convert a river's kinetic energy into electricity.

Hydroelectric Dam

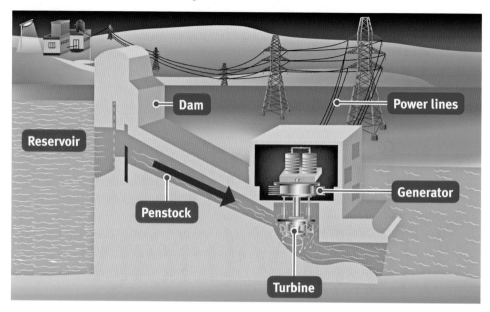

How It Works

When a dam is built across a river, it blocks the river's flow. This creates a **reservoir** of water. When gates on the back of the dam are opened, reservoir water flows into large pipes called penstocks. The rushing water passes through **turbines** at high speed. This spins the turbines, which in turn rotate the shaft of a **generator**. This produces electricity. Power lines carry the electricity to homes and businesses.

The amount of electricity a hydroelectric plant can produce depends mainly on two factors. One is the amount of water that passes through the turbines. The greater the flow of water, the more electricity can be produced. However, too much water flow can cause flooding or malfunctions in the dam. Hydroelectric power plants can adjust water flow by raising or lowering the gates on their dams.

Large dams often have several gates. Different ones can be opened at different times to better control the flow of water through the dam.

At more than 935 feet (285 m) tall, Switzerland's Grande Dixence Dam is among the tallest in the world.

The other factor that determines a hydroelectric plant's ability to produce electricity is the speed of the flowing water. Fast-flowing water produces more electricity. Tall dams are built to create a difference between the height of the reservoir water and the river below the dam. The farther the water falls through the penstocks, the faster it flows.

Storing Power

Pumped-storage systems collect water for hydroelectric plants to use during periods of high electricity demand. The first one was the Rocky River project. It was built by the Connecticut Light and Power Company and began operating in 1929. One of today's largest and most powerful pumped-storage plants is in Bath County, Virginia. Its six turbine generators are capable of pumping 14.5 million gallons (55 million liters) of water every minute!

A worker oversees the facilities inside the Bath County Pumped Storage Station in Virginia.

The Koepchenwerk Pumped-Storage Plant is located along the Ruhr River in Germany.

Pumped-storage plants have two reservoirs at different heights. When a power plant is producing more electricity than is needed, the extra is used to pump water from the lower reservoir to the upper reservoir. When more electricity is needed, water is released from the upper reservoir to operate the plant's turbines and generators.

The Three Gorges Dam

Located on China's Yangtze River, the Three Gorges Dam is the largest power plant ever built. The concrete and steel dam, one of the largest in the world, is 1.4 miles (2.3 km) long and 607 feet (185 meters) tall. Its power plant became fully functional in 2012 after a long construction process that began in 1994.

Many people opposed the dam's construction. Its reservoir flooded nearby towns and historic sites. Among these was one of China's natural wonders—the Three Gorges, for which the dam is named. Millions of people had to leave their homes. Many plant and animal species also lost their homes in the flooding.

Affecting the Environment

In many ways, hydropower can seem like the perfect energy source. Unlike power plants that burn fossil fuels, hydropower plants do not directly pollute the air. Unlike nuclear power plants, they do not create hazardous waste. Because of this, hydropower is known as a clean source of electricity. However, hydroelectricity can also cause its own environmental problems.

Losing Land

Hydropower reservoirs can flood thousands of acres. Often, this destroys farmland and wilderness. Local residents must abandon their homes. The flooding also threatens the survival of certain plants and animals.

A church lies underwater in Italy's Lake Reschen reservoir.

Overgrown algae turn water green.

Harmful Waters

Dams alter the health of rivers. Free-flowing rivers constantly refresh themselves as precipitation falls. But water in a reservoir slows to a standstill. It warms and **evaporates**. This increases the water's saltiness. **Algae** growth increases, depleting oxygen levels in the water. During power production, the reservoir's warm, oxygen-starved water enters the river below the dam. This can harm and kill river life far downstream.

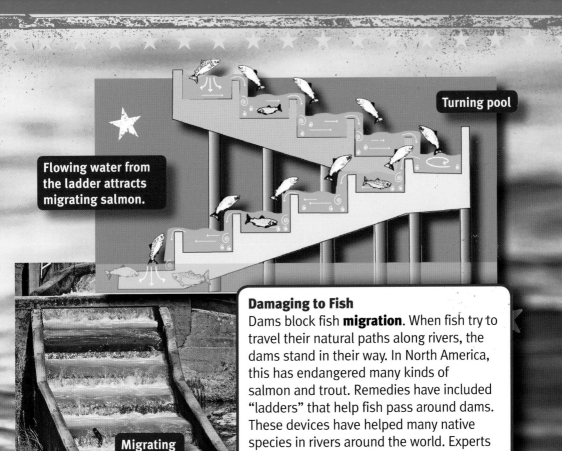

Turning pool

Flowing water from the ladder attracts migrating salmon.

Damaging to Fish

Dams block fish **migration**. When fish try to travel their natural paths along rivers, the dams stand in their way. In North America, this has endangered many kinds of salmon and trout. Remedies have included "ladders" that help fish pass around dams. These devices have helped many native species in rivers around the world. Experts continue to design other methods of helping migrating fish around dams.

Migrating salmon

Because of these kinds of issues, hundreds of dams have been removed from U.S. waterways since the 1990s. In these areas, fish populations that were once harmed by the dams have begun to grow again.

Ocean waves are full of kinetic energy as they rise and fall in the oceans.

CHAPTER 4

Tides and Waves

On ocean beaches around the world, many people love to watch as waves crash rhythmically against the coast. This beautiful movement of the water is caused by a combination of tidal movement and wind. Ocean levels rise and fall according to a regular cycle called the tide. The tide is caused mainly by the gravitational pull of the moon. Waves are formed as rising and falling ocean tides are pushed toward land by the wind. Today, the kinetic energy of tides and waves is being used to generate electricity.

Predictable Power

One thing that makes tidal power so useful is that we can predict when tides come and go. It is all based on the movement of the moon as it orbits Earth. This predictability gives tidal power a big advantage over other alternative energy sources. Wind power, solar power, and even the flow of rivers can be very unpredictable. We can never be sure when there will be plenty of power to generate electricity and when there won't be enough.

The amount of energy generated by a wind turbine can change a great deal from day to day or year to year.

The Moon's Effects

As the moon orbits Earth, its gravity pulls ocean water toward it. This causes a high tide. At the same time, another high tide forms all the way on the other side of the planet. This is because the moon's gravity pulls the entire planet toward it, away from the ocean on its opposite side. The water stays where it was, but the planet moves away. This causes the water level to rise in relation to ground levels. Low tides occur as the moon circles Earth, causing waters to fall as they are no longer pulled by its gravity.

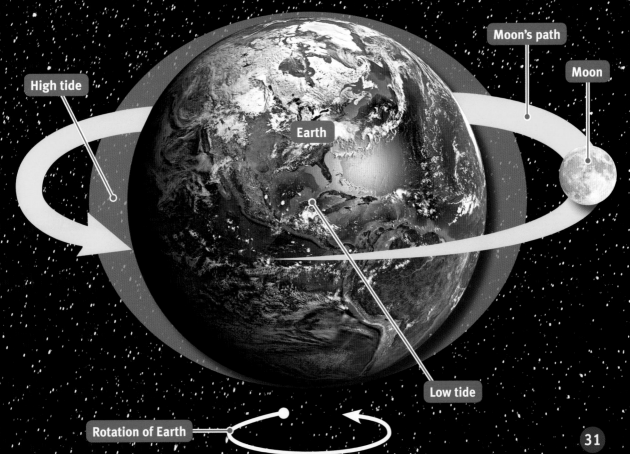

High tide

Moon's path

Moon

Earth

Low tide

Rotation of Earth

Tidal Barrage Power Plants

One way to capture the motion of tidal waters is called a tidal barrage power plant. A tidal barrage power plant is built across a narrow bay or river. When high tides raise the water level, gates at the power plant are closed to capture the water. At low tide, the water level outside the dam drops. The dam's gates are then opened. As the stored water falls downward, it propels turbines that generate electricity.

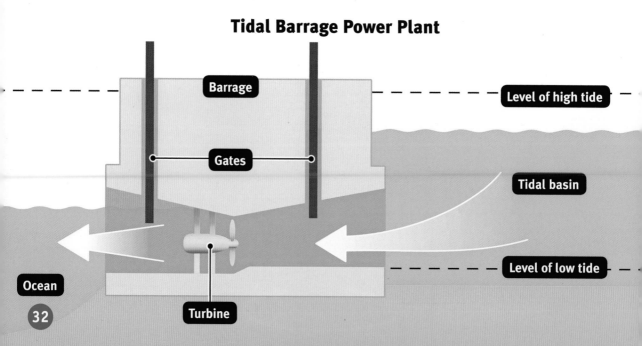

Tidal Barrage Power Plant

Barrage

Gates

Level of high tide

Tidal basin

Level of low tide

Ocean

Turbine

Tidal stream generators attached to the ocean floor end up looking much like an underwater version of a wind farm.

Underwater Turbines

Another method of capturing tidal power is the tidal stream generator (TSG). A TSG is an underwater turbine that looks like a submerged windmill. Its blades slowly rotate as the tides ebb and flow. TSGs have proved to be safe for wildlife in the water. Their blades move slowly enough for fish to swim between them. TSGs can be attached to the ocean floor or to structures such as bridges and dams.

Wave Farms

Ocean waves contain a tremendous amount of energy. Wave farms convert this wave energy into electricity. A wave farm consists of several large floating devices near each other in an area of ocean. The devices are often shaped like long cylinders. As waves hit them, they bob and move around. This motion pumps fluid into a generator that produces electricity. The power flows through a cable that is secured to the ocean floor.

Floating devices to capture wave energy have been tested off the coast of Scotland.

The Aguçadoura Wave Farm in Portugal was the world's first commercial wave farm. It opened in 2008. Its creators hoped it would provide power for 15,000 homes. However, a technical problem caused the farm to shut down.

Other similar projects have been proposed. The Wave Hub is being tested off the coast of Cornwall, England. It is the world's largest test site for offshore hydroelectric systems. Wave farms are also planned in Scotland, Spain, Italy, and Russia. In the United States, wave farms are in development off the coasts of New Jersey, Oregon, and Hawaii.

The hydroelectric plant in Hoover Dam is powered by 17 huge turbines.

CHAPTER 5

A Bright Future

Hydropower is the most widely used renewable energy source in the world. However, renewable sources only make up a small percentage of the world's total energy use. But many people are working to increase the use of clean, renewable energy. Hydropower will play a major role in this global effort.

Around the World

Hydropower is now produced in 150 countries. Overall, hydropower supplies about 16 percent of the world's electricity. However, it could one day provide even more than that. Only about one-third of all potential hydropower locations are currently in use. The United Nations has estimated that, if fully developed, hydropower could supply more than half of all the electricity used on Earth.

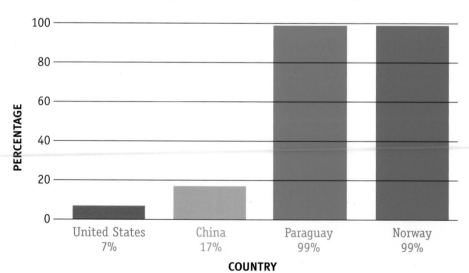

Hydropower Usage by Country

Norway: A Water Power Powerhouse

In Norway, a country in northern Europe, hydropower accounts for 99 percent of all energy production! The country's fast-flowing rivers are a primary source of hydropower. This nation is known for its efficient, environment-friendly, and beautiful hydropower plants. In fact, Norway has been called Europe's battery. It shares its extra electricity with the nearby countries of Denmark, Finland, the Netherlands, Sweden, and Russia.

A hydroelectric dam lies along the edge of Votna, a lake in southwestern Norway.

Water level during period of drought

Water level when rain is plentiful

Water levels in reservoirs such as Hoover Dam's Lake Mead can be reduced greatly by droughts.

A Changing Climate

In the coming years, climate change is expected to affect worldwide precipitation patterns. Some areas will receive less rainfall than usual. This will reduce river water flowing into hydropower plants, decreasing the amount of electricity we can generate from water. To counter this, experts are working to create turbines that work better at low water levels.

Other areas of the world are expected to receive more rainfall due to climate change. Hydropower plants could be very successful in such places.

Hydropower will never be able to meet the world's energy needs all on its own. There are also challenges associated with hydropower that still need to be solved. But along with other clean, renewable energy sources, such as solar, geothermal, and wind power, it can help cut down on the pollution caused by fossil fuels. Changing the way we get our energy can help make our world a greener, healthier place! ⭐

It took about seven years to build Turkey's Ermenek Dam.

Looking Back at the Book

What have you learned? Here's a quick review!
Can you add any details to the bits and pieces below?

PAGE 11

Forces that cause water to flow in rivers and streams

★ Gravity

★ Precipitation

PAGES 29–31

Forces that create tides and waves

★ The moon's orbit

★ Gravity

★ Wind

PAGES 13–17

Uses that people have found for hydropower

★ Irrigation

★ Transportation

★ Generating electricity

★ Telling time

★ Grinding grain

Irrigation

PAGES
19–24

Parts of a hydroelectric power plant

- ★ Dam
- ★ Reservoir
- ★ Power lines
- ★ Penstocks
- ★ Turbines
- ★ Generator

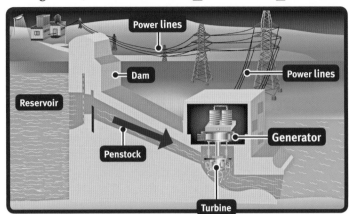

PAGE
32–35

Ways to capture power from waves and tides

True Statistics

Number of countries producing electricity generated from hydropower: 150

Percentage of world's electricity generated from hydropower: 16

Percentage of U.S. electricity generated from hydropower: 7

Percentage of Norway's electricity generated from hydropower: 99

Percentage of New Zealand's electricity generated from hydropower: 75

Length of the Three Gorges Dam: 1.4 mi. (2.3 km)

Number of lightbulbs lit by the first hydropower plant: 250

Number of people served by the Hoover Dam: 1.3 million

Did you find the truth?

F People first started using water power in the 1800s.

T Ocean waves are affected by the moon.

Resources

Books

Bethea, Nikole Brooks. *Building Dams*. Mendota Heights, MN: North Star Editions, 2017.

Doeden, Matt. *Finding Out About Hydropower*. Minneapolis: Lerner Publications Company, 2015.

Graham, Ian. *You Wouldn't Want to Work on the Hoover Dam! An Explosive Job You'd Rather Not Do*. New York: Franklin Watts, 2012.

Newman, Patricia. *Water Power*. Ann Arbor, MI: Cherry Lake Publishing, 2013.

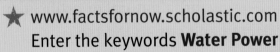

Visit this Scholastic website for more information on Water Power:
★ www.factsfornow.scholastic.com
Enter the keywords **Water Power**

Important Words

algae (AL-jee) small plants without roots or stems that grow mainly in water

axle (AK-suhl) a rod in the center of a wheel, around which the wheel turns

canals (kuh-NALZ) channels that are dug across land so that water can flow from one place to another

climate change (KLYE-mit CHAYNJ) global warming and other changes in the weather and weather patterns that are happening because of human activity

evaporates (i-VAP-uh-rayts) changes into a vapor or gas

generator (JEN-uh-ray-tur) a machine that produces electricity by turning a magnet inside a coil of wire

irrigation (ir-i-GAY-shuhn) the process of supplying water to crops by artificial means, such as channels and pipes

migration (mye-GRAY-shuhn) movement of people or animals from one region or habitat to another

renewable (rih-NOO-uh-buhl) coming from a source that is unable to be used up

reservoir (REZ-ur-vwahr) a natural or artificial lake in which water is collected and stored for use

turbines (TUR-buhnz) engines powered by water, steam, wind, or gas passing through the blades of a wheel and making it spin

Index

Page numbers in **bold** indicate illustrations.

About the Author

Laurie Brearley has written and edited numerous children's books and articles on a wide range of topics in science and social studies. She holds degrees from the University of New Hampshire and Boston University. Brearley believes that learning is a lifelong pursuit. She lives in Binghamton, New York, and is proud to be a descendant of David Brearley, one of the signers of the U.S. Constitution.